A Ticket to
Mexico

Tom Streissguth

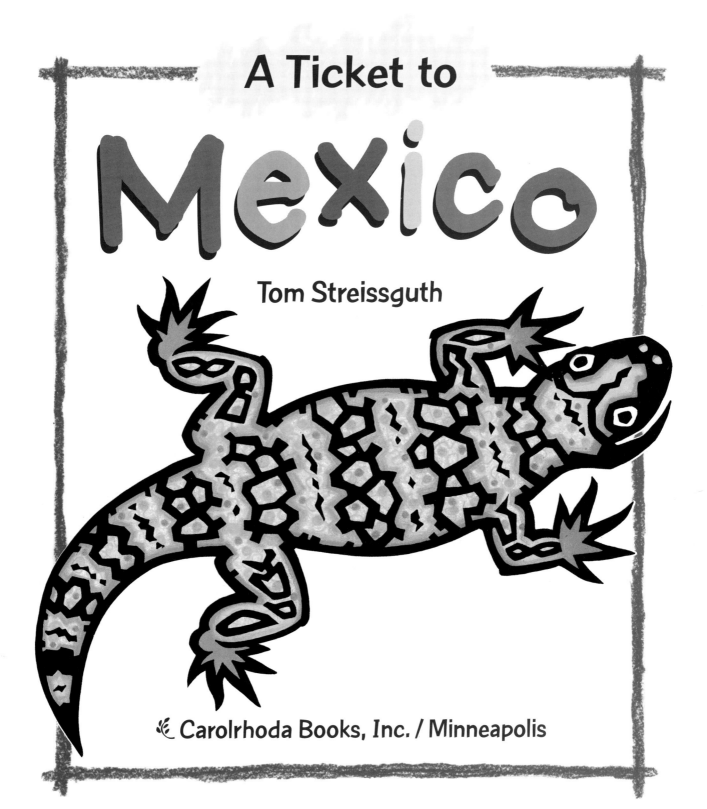

Carolrhoda Books, Inc. / Minneapolis

Photo Acknowledgments

Photos, maps, and artworks are used courtesy of: Laura Westlund, pp. 1, 2-3, 4, 7, 9, 27, 35, 41; © Nik Wheeler, pp. 5 (top), 10, 12, 13 (left and right), 16 (top), 18, 22, 26, 28, 30, 32, 34, 35, 38, 39 (left), 41, 42; © Mike Reed, pp. 5 (bottom), 23 (right), 45; David Mangurian, p. 6; © Chuck Place, pp. 6-7, 25, 27, 44; © Buddy Mays/TRAVEL STOCK, pp. 8, 9, 14 (left and middle), 15, 16 (bottom); John Erste, pp. 11, 13, 22, 24, 28, 32, 37; Paula Jansen, pp. 14 (right), 19, 20, 21, 33; Museum of Modern Art of Latin America, p. 17 (top); Phillips Bourns, p. 17 (bottom); © Monica V. Brown, pp. 18 (inset), 23 (left), 37; Tom Moran, pp. 24, 31, 40; Robert L. and Diane Wolfe, pp. 29, 43; Independent Picture Service, p. 36; Schalkwijk/Art Resource, NY, p. 39 (right). Cover photo of kindergartners from Guaymas by Paula Jansen.

Carolrhoda Books, Inc.
c/o The Lerner Publishing Group
241 First Avenue North
Minneapolis, Minnesota 55401 U.S.A.

Library of Congress Cataloging-in-Publication Data

Streissguth, Thomas, 1958-
  Mexico / by Tom Streissguth.
    p. cm. — (A ticket to)
  Includes index.
  Summary: Examines the geography, history, economy, society, and culture of Mexico.
  ISBN 1-57505-125-7 (lib. bdg. : alk. paper)
  1. Mexico—Juvenile literature. [1. Mexico.] I. Title. II. Series
F1208.5.S77   1997
972—dc 21   97-936

Manufactured in the United States of America
1 2 3 4 5 6 — SP — 02 01 00 99 98 97

Contents

All aboard! We're crossing a river called the
Rio Grande to the country of Mexico. At the
border, the river is called the Río Bravo del
Norte. Mexico sits on the **continent** of
North America. The United States lies north

of Mexico. Belize and Guatemala are south of Mexico. On a **map,** Mexico looks a bit like a giant ice-cream cone!

Can you find tropical rain forests (left) *and the Río Bravo* (below) *on the map?*

⛰	mountains
⣿	deserts
☰	plains
⼁⼁⼁	rain forests
∿	valleys
▲	volcanoes
★	country's capital
✶	canyon

Coast to Coast

Water is on almost every side of Mexico. The Pacific Ocean meets the country's long western coast. On the eastern side of Mexico lies a big circle of water called the Gulf of Mexico. Just about every kind of land can be found in Mexico. **Tropical rain forests, plains** (flat land),

There's a lot of water around Mexico for boating (right) *and playing* (above).

mountains, and dry **deserts** all cover Mexico. The country even has snow-covered mountaintops! Orizaba, Mexico's highest mountain, has snow on it year-round.

Map Whiz Quiz

Take a look at the map on page four. A map is a drawing or chart of a place. Trace the outline of Mexico onto a piece of paper. See if you can find the Pacific Ocean. Mark this side of your map with a "W" for west. How about the Gulf of Mexico? Mark this side with an "E" for east. Now color in the regions labeled Baja and Yucatán. These areas are called **peninsulas**—pieces of land with water on three sides.

Trains take Mexicans on long and short trips.

Traveling

There are fast ways and slow ways to travel in Mexico. Cars share the roads with trucks, buses, and sometimes donkeys! Trains go across plains and through **valleys.** Some farmers bring their crops to market on horse-drawn carts. Airplanes crisscross the

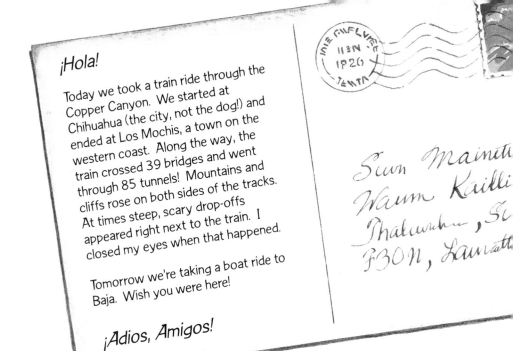

¡Hola!

Today we took a train ride through the Copper Canyon. We started at Chihuahua (the city, not the dog!) and ended at Los Mochis, a town on the western coast. Along the way, the train crossed 39 bridges and went through 85 tunnels! Mountains and cliffs rose on both sides of the tracks. At times steep, scary drop-offs appeared right next to the train. I closed my eyes when that happened.

Tomorrow we're taking a boat ride to Baja. Wish you were here!

¡Adios, Amigos!

Sun Mainet
Waum Kaithi
Thaluntu, St
730 N, Lauratt

This farmer uses cows to help move his stack of corn.

skies above. If you were in Mexico, what kind of ride would you choose?

In the Valley

In the middle of Mexico are two sets of mountains. One set is called the Western Sierra Madre. The other is known as the Eastern Sierra Madre. In between them lies a flat piece of land called the Valley of Mexico. The valley is

Millions of people live in Mexico City. It is the biggest city in the world!

home to Mexico City, the biggest city in the world. Long ago Aztec Indians also built cities in this valley. Then people from Spain crossed the Atlantic Ocean. They took over the Aztecs and their land. The Spaniards built their own cities.

An old story talks about the building of the city of Tenochtitlán by the Aztecs. They set up their city on the spot where they saw an eagle sitting on a cactus eating a snake. The eagle, the cactus, and the snake are pictured on the Mexican flag.

Snowy Popocatépetl

In the South

Giant twin **volcanoes** rise south of Mexico City. One is named Popocatépetl, which means "smoking mountain" in the Aztec language. The other volcano is Iztaccíhuatl,

Tasty mangoes

Spider monkeys live in Mexico's rain forests.

Wood from the rain forest

or "white woman." The Southern Sierra Madre stand south of the volcanoes. Nearby is a rain forest, where spider monkeys live. Mangoes and other fruits grow in the wet forest.

A cornseller from southern Mexico

A farmboy from Baja

Rollerbladers from Guaymas

Mexicans

At one time, Indians were the only people in Mexico. Then Spain took over. Many Spanish people moved to Mexico and married Indians. The children of these marriages are mestizos. The word *mestizo* means "mixed" in Spanish, the language of Spain. Most Mexicans are mestizos. Most people who make their homes in Mexico speak Spanish.

A boy in Mexico City carries flowers to market on his head.

Do you know what a pyramid is? Some of the oldest buildings in Mexico have a pyramid's shape. Early Indians, such as the Maya, put up the buildings. Many people visit the buildings every year.

First Peoples

Some parts of Mexico still have large numbers of Indians. The Maya, the Mixtec, and the Zapotec live in southern Mexico. In the dry northern states are the Seri, who move from

place to place
looking for food and
water. Some of
Mexico's Indians
speak little Spanish.
They use their own
languages.

Benito Juárez was a Zapotec Indian. He was president of Mexico at the same time that Abraham Lincoln—the man on the U.S. penny—was president of the United States.

This modern Mayan girl is wearing the style of clothing her great-great-grandparents wore.

Mexico City is crowded. Some people in the city cannot pay for nice homes, so they live in houses made of tin and wood.

Many People

Many Mexicans have nice places to live and plenty to eat, but other Mexicans are very poor. A lot of poor people live in Mexico

City. It's a very crowded place. Mexicans from small towns move to big cities because they want to find jobs. Some people leave Mexico altogether.

To find a better life, some Mexicans seek work in the United States. This move is risky. If the jobseekers do not have permission to live in the neighboring country, they can be sent back to Mexico.

Not everyone in Mexico is poor. Some Mexicans live in nice houses and get plenty of food.

Family

Family life is very important in Mexico. Mexican households can be very large. Many have three, four, or more children. Families sometimes share their home with relatives—aunts, uncles, cousins, and grandparents. Grandparents help

A sunny day at the beach brings together the whole family.

All in the Family

Here are the Spanish words for family members.

father	padre	(PAH-dray)
mother	madre	(MAH-dray)
uncle	tío	(TEE-oh)
aunt	tía	(TEE-ah)
grandfather	abuelo	(ah-BWAY-loh)
grandmother	abuela	(ah-BWAY-lah)
son	hijo	(EE-hoh)
daughter	hija	(EE-hah)
brother	hermano	(ehr-MAH-noh)
sister	hermana	(ehr-MAH-nah)

with chores and watch the children. Grown-up sons and daughters take care of family members as they get older.

Some houses in Mexico sit close to the street.

Neighborhoods

The streets in Mexican cities are lively. *¡Hola!* People shout as they say hello to their friends on the sidewalks. Honk! Cars, buses, and motor scooters rush past on the road. Home is a good place to get away from all the noise. Some Mexican homes are made of

stone, with quiet courtyards in the center. Many city families live in tall apartment buildings. In Mexican towns and villages, houses

are usually made of adobe clay bricks. In Yucatán the Maya Indians build small homes out of tree branches and grass.

The Maya build their houses (above) of grass and tree branches. Brick houses (left) may be painted in pretty colors.

23

This girl is mixing chocolate to make hot chocolate for breakfast. What do you have for breakfast?

Food

¡Caliente! Mexican food is hot. That's what caliente means. Thanks to the chile pepper, eating south of the border can be a spicy adventure.

Meet Señor Chile Pepper—that dude is hot!

24

A farmer shows off an ear of corn. Corn is an important food in Mexico. Corn is made into tortillas and other tasty foods.

Did You Know?

Avocadoes, tomatoes, potatoes, peanuts, and chile peppers grow well in Mexico's hot, sunny climate. These foods are native to Mexico. That means these foods have always been grown there.

Folks in Mexico have been growing chile peppers and other foods such as corn for thousands of years. The tortilla—a thin, flat cornmeal pancake—is served with every meal, just like bread.

You can buy almost any thing at a Mexican market.

Market

Mexicans shop at outdoor markets. The markets open early and stay open all day long. Shoppers can buy food, clothing, jewelry—almost everything they need. In small towns, farmers bring their extra crops to sell at the local market. They weigh the

A taco stand at the market

fruits and vegetables on a scale for customers. The farmers may also have chickens, ducks, or turkeys for sale.

In Mexico some people chain their pet iguanas to keep them from running away—much the way you would tie up a dog. Can you imagine a lizard on a leash?

People in Mexico put on special clothing during parties called fiestas.

Fiesta!

In Mexico a special party is called a fiesta. During a fiesta, school closes and work stops. Everyone in town meets at the plaza for a fun time. Bands play. People laugh, sing, and wave to their friends. Piñatas— decorated pots filled with candy—are hung from trees or ceilings. Blindfolded children take turns trying to smash open the piñata with a wooden stick. People shout and fireworks go off. The celebration may last for a full day or even two! Nobody gets much sleep during a fiesta.

Day of the Dead

Every year, on November 2, Mexicans celebrate the Day of the Dead. This holiday is a time to remember family members who have died. Families create offerings of food and flowers to honor these relatives. At night the family brings candles and sets up a picnic near their relatives' graves. But the Day of the Dead isn't sad. It's a celebration!

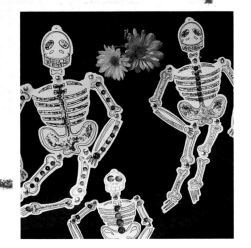

Most Mexican children wear uniforms to school. Do you?

School

Mexican children start school at age six. Many Mexican schools have new equipment, such as computers. But other schools, especially in poor areas, have very little besides a room and desks. In these parts of

Mexico, some children don't go to school at all or go for just a few years. These kids need to work at home or on their family's farm.

A Day Like Yours?

Paula María Fosada is 10 years old and goes to school in southern Mexico. Each morning her mother walks her to school, where Paula María studies from 8:00 to 1:00. In the afternoon, Paula María finishes her homework and does a few chores before she is allowed to play. Does Paula María's day sound like yours?

Some fiestas begin with everyone going to church. Then the people walk in parades.

Faith and Fiestas

Most people in Mexico belong to the Roman Catholic Church. This was the church of the Spanish settlers. But some Indians have other religious beliefs. The Tarahumara people worship the spirits of the sun, the moon, and the rain. The Maya and the Zapotec also practice old customs and beliefs.

December 12

December 12 is an important date in Mexico. On that day, Catholics honor the Virgin of Guadalupe. On December 12 in the year 1531, an Indian named Juan Diego had a vision of the Virgin Mary, the mother of Jesus. A church has been built on the spot in Mexico City where Juan Diego saw the Virgin. People who cannot travel to the church celebrate the day with a fiesta in their own hometown.

Games

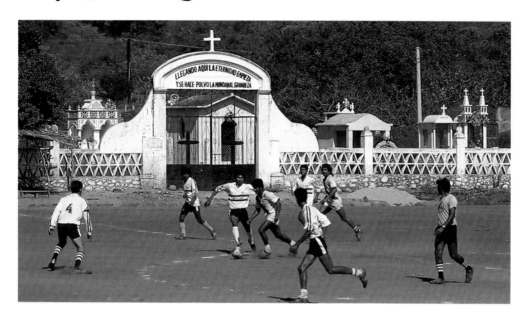

Soccer players

Mexicans love soccer! In Spanish, it's called *fútbol.* Adults and children play fútbol. They choose sides and set up goals in the streets, on playgrounds, and in soccer fields.

Bullfighting is also well liked. Many Mexican towns have a bullring. Mexico City has the largest bullring in the world. It's called the

Bullfighting

Baseball

Many Mexicans are baseball fans. Sometimes players from Mexican teams join the U.S. major leagues. Fernando Valenzuela is a popular Mexican-born pitcher. Mexicans call him "El Toro" (the Bull). Valenzuela pitches for the San Diego Padres. Other Mexican-born players are New York Mets pitcher Armando Reynoso, Colorado Rockies infielder Vinny Castilla, and Los Angeles Dodgers pitcher Ismael Valdés. What's your favorite team?

Plaza de México and has enough seats for 50,000 people. You can buy a ticket for a seat in the shade or a seat in the sun. Seats in the sun cost less.

Story Time

Mexico is a land of storytellers. Long ago the Maya and the Aztecs used pictures to tell stories. In 1539 the first printing press in

A Mexican bookshop

Mexico began making books in Mexico City. Since then Mexico has made many different kinds of books.

An Aztec Tale

Would you like to hear a very old Aztec story? This tale explains how the Aztecs came to be. A long time ago, all the world's human beings were killed in a flood. Later the Aztec god Quetzalcoatl tricked the god who took care of the dead into giving him the bones of the dead. Quetzalcoatl ground the bones into a powder and mixed them with his own blood to create the Aztecs.

This is a mural, or very big wall painting, of the Mexican hero Father Miguel Hildalgo.

Pictures

Another way of telling a story is through paintings. Murals are huge paintings on walls or ceilings. Three well-known painters—José Clemente Orozco, David Alfaro Siqueiros, and Diego Rivera—created many murals on

Frida Kahlo

Frida Kahlo was a Mexican artist who made colorful paintings of herself. Here she is in one of her works. Can you find the monkey?

Schoolchildren often visit places with murals to learn about Mexico's history.

the walls of important buildings in Mexico. By studying the murals, a person can learn about Mexico's past.

Music and Dance

Charras, *or female riders, and* **charros,** *male riders, do a Mexican dance.*

Because the weather in Mexico is warm year-round, Mexicans spend much of their time outside. In some towns, a concert takes place on Sunday nights in the plaza. A street band plays Mexican folk music. Band members dress in *charro* clothing, the traditional cowboy outfit.

Flying Dancers

The Totonac Indians, who live near the Gulf of Mexico, do an ancient ceremony called the Voladores. The Voladores has four men who have ropes wound around their waists. The ends of the ropes are tied to the top of a high pole. The four men jump head first from the tower. No kidding! The tower spins around, the ropes unwind, and the men slowly dance and twist their way down to the ground. At the last minute, they turn rightside-up and land on their feet. What an amazing flight!

Guitar players take a break.

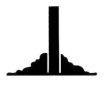

41

Crafts

Artists in Mexico make crafts by hand to sell on the streets, in the plazas, and at the marketplace. Potters, weavers, jewelers, basket makers, painters, and

Indians weaving cloth

wood-carvers create traditional pots, rugs, necklaces, kitchen tools, and wall hangings. Some cities are known for a certain craft. People in the southern city of Puebla make brightly painted tiles for decorating buildings.

Craftworks

A *papel picado* is a brightly colored paper with cutout designs. Several are strung together as decorations for fiestas in Mexico. Making a papel picado is fun. All you need is tissue paper and a pair of scissors. But don't forget! Scissors can be sharp, so ask an adult for some help. Here's what you do:

1. Take a sheet of tissue paper that measures 30 inches by 20 inches. Cut it into four equally sized pieces. Each piece will be 15 inches by 10 inches.
2. Fold one of the pieces in half the short way. Fold the paper in half two more times.
3. Cut away sections from the folded edges to form a design. Be careful not to cut all the way from one edge to the other. The paper will fall apart!
4. Repeat these steps to the other three pieces. Unfold them. Glue or staple one edge of each papel picado to a long piece of string so they hang in a row.

A Mayan statue

New Words to Learn

continent: Any one of seven large areas of land. The continents are Africa, Antarctica, Asia, Australia, Europe, North America, and South America.

desert: A dry, sandy region.

earthquake: A shaking of the ground caused by the shifting of underground rock.

hurricane: A big storm with strong winds and heavy rain.

map: A drawing or chart of all or part of the earth or sky.

mestizo: A person who has one Spanish parent and one Native American parent.

mountain: A part of the earth's surface that rises high into the sky.

peninsula: A piece of land that has water on three of its sides. The fourth side is connected to land.

plain: A large area of flat land.

tropical rain forest: A thick, green forest that gets lots of rain every year.

Girls strolling after school

valley: A low-lying piece of land between hills or moutains. Valley can also mean an area of land that gets its water from a large river.

volcano: An opening in the earth's surface through which hot, melted rock shoots up. Volcano can also mean the hill or mountain of ash and rock that builds up around the opening.

New Words to Say

Baja	BAH-hah
Belize	beh-LEEZ
Benito Juarez	bay-NEE-toh WAH-rays
caliente	kah-lee-EHN-tay
Chiapas	chee-AHP-ahs
chinas poblanas	CHEE-nahs poh-BLAH-nahs
David Alfaro Siqueiros	dah-VEED ahl-FAHR-oh see-KAY-rohs
hola	OH-lah
Iztaccíhuatl	ees-tahk-SEE-wahtl
José Clemente Orozco	hoh-SAY klay-MAYN-tay oh-ROHS-koh
José Guadalupe Posada	hoh-SAY gwah-dah-LOO-pay poh-SAH-dah
papel picado	pah-PELL pee-KAH-doh
Popocatépetl	poh-poh-kah-TEH-pehtl
Puebla	PWAY-blah
Quetzalcoatl	keht-SAHL-kwahtl
Sierra Madre	see-EHR-rah MAH-dray
Volodores	voh-lah-DOH-rehs
Yucatán	yuh-kuh-TAHN

More Books to Read

Haskins, Jim. *Count Your Way Through Mexico.* Minneapolis: Carolrhoda Books, Inc., 1989.

Irizarry, Carmen. *Passport to Mexico.* New York: Franklin Watts, Inc., 1994.

Keller, Mary J. *Mexico Activity Book: Arts, Crafts, Cooking & Historical Aids.* San Juan Capistrano, CA: Edupress, 1996.

Maitland, Katherine. *Ashes for Gold: A Tale from Mexico.* Greenvale, NY: Mondo Publishing, 1994.

Moran, Tom. *A Family in Mexico.* Minneapolis: Lerner Publications Company, 1987.

Olawsky, Lynn Ainsworth. *Colors of Mexico.* Minneapolis: Carolrhoda Books, Inc., 1997.

Silverthorne, Elizabeth. *Fiesta!: Mexico's Great Celebrations.* Brookfield, CT: The Millbrook Press, 1992.

Staub, Frank. *Children of the Sierra Madre.* Minneapolis: Carolrhoda Books, Inc., 1996.

Staub, Frank. *Children of the Yucatan.* Minneapolis: Carolrhoda Books, Inc., 1996.

Tabor, Nancy M. *A Taste of the Mexican Market.* Watertown, MA: Charlesbridge Publishing, Inc., 1996.

Temko, Florence. *Traditional Crafts from Mexico and Central America.* Minneapolis: Lerner Publications Company, 1996.

Wolf, Bernard. *Beneath the Stone: A Mexican Zapotec Tale.* New York: Orchard Books, 1994.

New Words to Find